The Story of
Caves

Revised Edition

by DOROTHY STERLING

Illustrated with photographs
Drawings by WINIFRED LUBELL

SCHOLASTIC BOOK SERVICES

Published by Scholastic Book Services, a division
of Scholastic Magazines, Inc., New York, N. Y.

1st printing .... September 1966

Printed in the U.S.A.

ACKNOWLEDGMENTS

The author would like to thank Mr. Charles Mohr for his many suggestions and for his careful reading of the manuscript. Mr. Mohr is a past president of the National Speleological Society, director of the Kalamazoo (Michigan) Nature Center, and a member of the lecture staff of the Audubon Society.

Thanks are also due Dr. Junius Bird, Curator of South American Archaeology, American Museum of Natural History, for reading the chapter on "Cave Men."

Other books by Dorothy Sterling:

Caterpillars
Creatures of the Night
Insects and the Homes They Build
The Story of Mosses, Ferns, and Mushrooms
Spring Is Here
Fall Is Here
Mary Jane*

* Available through Scholastic Book Services

Contents

Introduction

The Underworld

Long ago in the land of Greece, a boy named Dion scrambled up the rocky slope at the edge of a pasture. From the top of a big boulder he could see the sheep nibbling grass in the meadow below. The sun was warm, and he stretched out on the flat rock. He wasn't going to sleep. He was just going to lie back and watch the clouds as they sailed slowly across the sky. He wasn't going to sleep. He was just going to close his eyes.

"Yip, yip, yip!"

Dion awakened with a start. He knew that noise. It was Argos, the sheep dog, barking to tell him that something was wrong. Sliding down the rock, Dion ran toward his flock.

"Thirteen, fourteen," he counted as he ran. Sure enough, one of the sheep was missing. The little black lamb, baby of the flock, was nowhere to be seen.

"Yip, yip, yip!" Argos kept on barking until Dion patted his head and breathlessly asked, "What's wrong? What's the matter, old boy?"

As the dog stood there with his ears cocked and his tail wagging, Dion could hear a faint, faraway bleat. It came from under the ground. In front of Argos, between two big rocks, a hole led down into the earth. The little black lamb had stumbled into the hole. Now it couldn't make its way out again.

What should Dion do?

The lamb bleated again. It sounded farther away now. If Dion were going to save it, he must crawl into the hole without waiting another minute.

But he couldn't. He just couldn't go into that dark hole. Dion could climb the tallest trees and jump from the highest rocks. He could swim farther and run faster than any boy he knew. There wasn't anything on earth that he was afraid of.

But he was afraid of the world *under* the earth — of the world that his people believed existed there. Afraid of Pluto, the dark-bearded god who was supposed to rule the underworld. Afraid of the inky River Styx and Cerberus, the three-headed dog with the tail of a snake, who guarded Pluto's palace. Afraid of the dead whose groans and shrieks echoed through Pluto's land. Afraid that, once he set foot in Pluto's damp and sunless kingdom, he would never return to the world of warmth and light.

So it was that Dion came home at dusk with only fourteen sheep in the flock. And because his parents shared his fears, they praised their son instead of scolding him.

"I would rather sacrifice my whole flock than have you enter Pluto's kingdom," his father said, while his mother built a fire on the altar in the courtyard to give thanks to the gods for her son's safe return.

In ancient Greece it wasn't only the shepherds and their sons who feared the world under the earth. Even the wise men were afraid of the dark caverns, and thought that the echoing cave noises and roaring underground streams were caused by gods and magic.

In other countries, different kinds of stories were told about caves. If Dion had been a Norwegian boy, he would have been sure that his lamb had been stolen by the trolls. Trolls were supposed to be misshapen creatures, sometimes giants and sometimes gnomes, who lived in caves and dug from mines the precious stones that were buried there. The palaces of the troll kings were said to be decorated with gold and silver, and their thrones to sparkle with rubies and diamonds.

From the east came still another tale about the underworld. Perhaps you remember Ali Baba, the poor woodcutter who watched a band of thieves hide their loot in a cave in the woods. After they had gone, he cried, "Open sesame!" The door of the cave swung open, and Ali Baba carried away the sacks of gold and silver that the thieves had hidden there.

Stories of treasure hidden in caves have been told in every country right down to modern times. Aladdin wriggled through a narrow cave passageway to discover his magic lamp in a palace under the earth in China. And Tom Sawyer and Huck Finn found an ironbound box filled with gold coins in McDougal's Cave in Missouri.

Probably you have heard or read of other cave tales. But have you ever wondered about the true story of caves? When were these mysterious holes in the ground formed? Who has lived in them? What is life underground really like?

Today men and women explore this underground world with steel ladders and nylon ropes and aqualungs. They light up the inky blackness with electricity and use rubber boats to ford the underground streams. They have solved the mystery of the hollowed-out rocks, and they are studying the paths of the roaring, echoing rivers. They are learning the story of cave animals and cave men. There really *is* treasure buried in caves. But it is very different from the treasure that Ali Baba found!

Chapter 1

Before Caves

IMAGINE THAT IT IS JANUARY 1, 300,000,000 B.C.
You are visiting North America. The sun is shining, and it's warm. But you shiver a little as you look around, because nothing seems familiar.

Looking at the landscape from the air, you search in vain for the White Mountains and the Rockies, the Mississippi River and the Grand Canyon, or the great plains of the Middle West. No sign of them! Here and there you see some islands, but most of the continent-to-be is covered by the sea.

You want to explore, so you wade through the shallow waters of the sea. Now you notice seaweeds and jellyfish floating near the surface, while awkward, crablike creatures slowly crawl along the sandy bottom. You stub your toe on something and reach down to pick it up. It's a shell, shaped like an overgrown ice-cream cone. When the animal that lives inside pokes out long feelers, you quickly drop it.

But there are other smaller shells, and you wish you had brought along a pail to carry some home with you. Here are spiral shells, not very different from the snails you found on the beach last summer. Here are fan-shaped shells with scalloped edges. Here are double shells that remind you of clams and mussels. On the back of some of these are curving tubes in which sea worms hide.

The prettiest of all these shells looks like a plant. But inside, tiny creatures too small to be seen without a magnifying glass have built rooms, one on top of the other. As you break off a brittle branch, you realize that you've found coral.

All of these animals — from the creature in its pointed cone to the tiny animals that build coral — are doing something completely new. They are taking lime that's dissolved in the sea water and building it into hard-shell homes.

"Lime," you wonder. "Like lime lollipops and limeade?"

No. The lime flavoring you're thinking of comes from a green fruit the size and shape of a lemon. The lime that the sea animals build with is a mineral whose scientific name is *calcium carbonate,* or *calcite.* Chalk is made of calcium carbonate. So are eggshells and human bones.

Shell homes were important for the slow-moving, soft-bodied animals of the ancient seas. Shells protected these animals from enemies that lurked under the seaweed or that swam swiftly through the clear water.

These shell homes are the beginning of the story of caves. They became the special kind of rock in which caves are formed.

It's time to skip ahead a million years or so. All kinds of things have been happening to our continent. The earth's crust has shrunk, cracked, wrinkled. The tops of the wrinkles have become mountains. Rivers now flow in the cracks and the creases.

More great changes are going on. The rivers wear away the rocky tops of the mountains. They grind rocks into stones, and stones into pebbles, and pebbles into sand and clay. Then they spread the sand and clay in the valleys and carry it away to the oceans' shores.

The shallow seas are becoming marshy plains. Where tiny animals once built their delicate coral homes underwater, there are now land plants stretching their roots in soil, and land animals stretching their necks to nibble at the plants' green leaves.

Fan-shaped shell (above) and coral (below) left by animals of the ancient seas. Limestone is made from such shells.

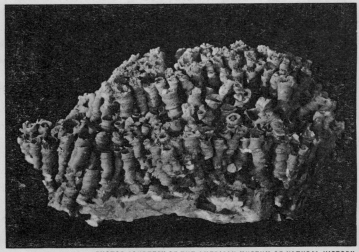

But what happened to all the animals of the ancient seas — the ones with cone-shaped shells, the sea worms and the coral builders, the snail-like, clamlike creatures of the shallow waters? Did they vanish without a trace?

No. They're buried under the soil, under the marshy plains. But they *have* changed.

As these animals died, their hard-shell homes sank to the bottom of the sea. Shells piled on top of shells. The cone-shaped shells and the spirals and the shells that looked like clams. The hard tubes of the sea worms and the hard coral. Millions of shells, billions of shells, shells beyond counting.

Slowly these shells piled up, only to be buried in turn by more shells. Those on the bottom of the pile were slowly crushed into bits by the weight of those above. Some shells remained whole, but were cemented to the tiny particles that surrounded them. In this way the layers of shells were crushed and pressed together, until finally, after millions of years, they hardened into rock — a special kind of rock known as *limestone*.

And limestone is the kind of rock in which most caves are formed.

Chapter 2

How Caves Begin

Y OU STUB YOUR TOE against a door. "Ouch!" you holler. "That door's as hard as rock."

But just how hard *is* rock?

That's a question that can't be answered by saying "ten pounds hard" or "twenty feet hard" or even "very hard." There are rocks that you can crumble in your hand or cut with a knife. There are rocks that can be broken with an ordinary hammer. And there are rocks too hard to break with a hammer. If you've ever watched men building a road, you have seen them boring into rock with pneumatic drills. Sometimes the rock is too hard even for these powerful pointed drills, and the workmen have to blow it to bits with dynamite.

The fact is that rocks differ greatly in their hardness. Limestone is one of the softer rocks. You can scratch it with a nail or a coin. Granite is one of the hardest rocks. But even the toughest, most solid chunk of granite won't last forever. And its chief enemy isn't dynamite. Its chief enemy is water!

Water can eat away the hardest rock. Water can wear down the tops of mountains. Water can crumble cliffs and grind up boulders. Water can hollow out the sides of hills as surely — though not as quickly — as any dynamite charge.

"Waterfalls," you suggest. "Roaring flood waters. Rushing streams. Pounding waves."

Yes, of course. But even a gentle stream can eat away "soft" rock. So can water under the ground, the water we tap when we drill a well, the same water we drink. This happens slowly, very slowly. It may take hundreds of thousands of years for the water to eat out, to dissolve, a big cave.

It can happen a little faster when the water is mildly acid. One of the special things about limestone is that the lime of which it is made is *soluble* in acid. That is, lime dissolves in acid, just as salt dissolves in water or sugar in hot cocoa.

The particular acid that works on limestone comes from the air and from the soil. Falling rain absorbs a gas called *carbon dioxide* from the atmosphere. As the drops of rain sink through the soil, they gather more carbon dioxide from the decaying plants and animals. Rain water containing carbon dioxide becomes *carbonic acid*.

When you hear the word "acid," what do you think of? Vinegar? Sulphuric acid? Something sour and strong and probably poisonous? Carbonic acid isn't like that at all. It's weak and pleasant-tasting. In fact, so pleasant that you often taste it. Whenever you drink club soda or ginger ale, you're drinking carbonic acid. The bubbles that fizz as you uncap the bottle are bubbles of carbon dioxide.

It's strange to think of ordinary soda water as a powerful substance. Yet this weak acid tunnels along cracks in the limestone, making them wider and wider. This acid rain water hollows out great caverns under the earth. Sometimes it fills these caverns with fantastic and beautiful rock formations.

Whenever it rains, drops of water soak through the soil. Some water is taken up by the plants that grow there. Some water runs off, feeding streams and rivers. Some of the water soaks into the ground. Where there are buried beds of limestone, this rain water begins its work of dissolving the limestone.

How? First the water trickles into tiny cracks in the limestone, making them larger. The cracks widen into crevices. The crevices enlarge into channels and tunnels. The tunnels meet, crisscross, and become as large as rooms. The rain water is now an underground river that fills the tunnels and floods the stone-walled rooms.

The level of the underground rivers is about the same as that of the rivers you see above the ground. (This water level is called the *water table*.) As rivers cut deeper, both under and above the ground, the water table sinks lower and lower. If a valley is cut deep enough and the river level becomes very low, the water will drain out of nearby caves like water out of a bathtub, leaving the caves high and dry. The caves won't be completely dust-dry, because rain water still runs through them. But most of the water keeps on draining until it reaches the new, lower water level. If there's more limestone

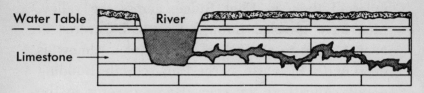

Water fills riverbed and caves below water level.

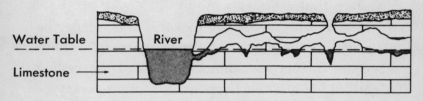

Water drains from caves as water table goes down.

below, the cave will keep on growing — to giant size — as long as the rock layers are under water.

It is difficult to realize just how much rock has been dissolved and carried away. In western Kentucky and across the Ohio River in Indiana, there are caves with thousands of miles of passages, side by side, sometimes in four or five layers. Stretched end to end, these underground passages would circle the earth a couple of times. Yet you will seldom see surface streams in this area. Rain sinks down through the rock crevices to swell underground rivers.

Mammoth Cave in Kentucky has forty-four miles

of mapped passageways, and there are forty more miles of them in Flint Ridge, across the valley. Men have traveled through Carlsbad Caverns in New Mexico to a depth of 1,076 feet — almost as deep under the earth as the Empire State Building is tall! And there are even deeper caverns in the mountains of France and Spain, in Mexico and the western United States.

A cave can grow so big that it will no longer be a cave. As the water eats away the rock, ceilings become thinner and thinner. Parts of the ceiling "cave-in." When this happens, only an arch may be left standing — all that remains of an ancient cave. Such arches are called "natural bridges."

Where large areas of limestone are exposed and rainfall is heavy, an entire countryside may be "destroyed." This is what has happened in the Karst region of Yugoslavia, where cracks in the surface of the rock were enlarged into *sinkholes*. These are shaped like sunken bowls hundreds of feet deep and often half a mile across. The cave roofs collapsed, and the caves became valleys, exposed to wind and rain. The word "karst" is now used to describe this kind of barren landscape wherever it occurs. In this country, there are karst regions in the limestone areas of Kentucky, Tennessee, Indiana, and Florida.

Chapter 3

Decorating a Cave

A SINGLE DROP OF WATER clings to the ceiling of the cave. Slowly, in the dry air of the cave, it evaporates. The drop of water disappears, leaving behind a tiny circle of lime.

What is happening?

Do you remember that lime dissolves in acid, just as salt does in water? When something dissolves, it isn't destroyed. It's still there, in the solution, even though you can't see it.

If you stir a tablespoon of salt into a glass of warm water, the salt becomes invisible. But when you heat the mixture on the stove until the water evaporates, there will still be salt in the pot — the same amount of salt that you started with.

The acid rain water dissolves the lime. The water carries the lime along with it as it travels down through the rock. When it reaches a cave room where the air is comparatively dry, the water evaporates, leaving behind its burden of lime. The lime becomes visible, just as the salt in the pot did. This is what happened to that single drop of water clinging to the ceiling of the cave.

Now a second raindrop deposits lime in the same place. Then comes a third drop and a fourth, until over the years, over the centuries, the crumbs of lime grow into hard stone icicles. These are the formations known as *stalactites*.

Young stalactites are usually hollow. You can stand underneath one and actually drink the drops of water that drip through this stone straw. After a while the hollow center is filled in. Now the stalactite grows from the outside. It continues to grow as long as drops of water trickle down its surface.

How fast does a stalactite grow? That varies from cave to cave, depending on the amount of rainfall, the thickness of the limestone beds, and the dryness of the cave air. Some stalactites grow an inch a year, others less than an inch in a century. Stalactites are made up of rings of lime, one outside the other, like the rings in the trunk of a tree.

Not all of the drops of water evaporate from the ceiling of the cave. Some splash to the floor where they build a *stalagmite*. (If you have trouble remembering which is which, think of the c in stalactite as standing for "ceiling" and the g in stalagmite as standing for "ground.")

Above two huge stalagmites hang many small stalactites

Stalagmites usually have a broader base and a blunter tip than the stalactites. Sometimes their tops are hollowed out like cups. Drops of water splashing into the cup spatter bits of lime along the side of the stalagmite. If a stalactite reminds you of an icicle, a stalagmite often makes you think of a candle with melted wax dripping down. But this candle is of stone, and it's growing larger instead of melting.

Some stalagmites grow to enormous size. In Carlsbad Caverns, New Mexico, there are stalagmites fifteen feet across the base and more than sixty-five feet high — as wide as a room and taller than a six-story building. Others may be only inches wide but many feet tall.

Often the stalactite growing from the ceiling and the stalagmite growing from the floor meet to form a *column*. Sometimes such columns almost fill the cave rooms.

As water slowly trickles down cave walls, it builds another kind of formation, a ripply stone surface known as *flowstone*. Flowstone starts as a thin coating on the wall and floor of the cave. When layer after layer is added, it looks like a waterfall — a frozen Niagara.

A "waterfall" of flowstone

Two giant columns. The one on the left is mostly stalagmite and that on the right, stalactite.

In many caves, water seeps through long cracks in the ceiling to form wavy curtains. These *dripstone* formations may grow from ceiling to floor until the stone drapery actually divides the cave room in two. Or they may hang down in ribbonlike strips, looking like nothing more romantic than broad slabs of bacon.

Pools on the floor of the cave are often edged with

lacy films of lime known as *rimstone,* and thin lime pancakes float on the surface of the water. When the pancakes grow larger, they sink to the bottom of the pool to break up into coral-like pebbles.

In a shallow pool, the lime may fasten itself to single grains of sand. As water slowly drips into the pool, the grains turn round and round. New layers of lime are added, and the sand grains become *cave pearls.* The pearls grow until they are too heavy to be turned by the water. If you were

CARLSBAD CAVERNS, NATIONAL PARK SERVICE PHOTO

MAMMOTH ONYX CAVE, KY., PHOTO BY W. T. AUSTIN

Delicate crystal decorations found only on certain rare cave ceilings: helectites *(above)* and anthodites *(right).*

SKYLINE CAVERNS, VA., PHOTO

to cut through a cave pearl — its scientific name is *oölite* — you would see thin layers of stone, like the layers of an onion, with a tiny core in the center.

One of the most beautiful cave formations is the *helictite,* a twisted stalactite whose crystal branches often curl up or down or sideways, defying the laws of gravity. Scientists still do not agree on how they are able to grow in this fashion.

Equally beautiful are the *anthodites,* thin crystal needles found in clusters on cave ceilings. These fragile white spikes are a rare form of stalactite, found in a few caves in Virginia's Shenandoah Valley. An anthodite is believed to grow only one inch in seven thousand years!

Sometimes water traveling down to the cave dissolves and leaves behind other substances besides limestone. In many Kentucky caves, there are curving stone feathers and flowers that look like tiger lilies and roses. These cave flowers are made of *gypsum,* a white mineral that is softer than limestone.

Not all of the cave formations can be named and classified. The busy drops of water work with whatever materials they can find. Did an Indian moccasin leave a print on the muddy floor of a cave before Columbus' time? The print is still there, preserved by the lime that covers it. Did a soldier carve his initials on a cave wall during Civil War days? His initials can still be seen under their limey coating. Did a cave explorer leave a lantern behind? No use for him to pick it up when he returns a few years later — it's cemented to the floor, forever a part of the cave.

The cave will shine, and even sparkle, as long as there is water dripping from the ceiling and trickling along the walls. Only when all water is blocked off from the underground rooms, only then will the cave lose its luster and become dull and dingy.

Chapter 4

How to Find a Cave

How to Find a Cave

THOUSANDS OF UNKNOWN CAVES are waiting to be discovered. And cave detectives are hunting for them. They look for clues like limestone rock, sinkholes and disappearing streams, and currents of air coming from holes in the ground.

Skyline Caverns in Virginia were discovered by a scientist who hunted for six months in the foothills of the Blue Ridge Mountains until he found what he was looking for: an opening in a limestone ledge that led to the cave below. He had gathered so many clues that he *knew* a cave was there before he started to hunt. All he had to do was to find it!

Most caves have not been discovered in this way. Almost all of the well-known American caverns have been found by accident — and often it was a boy or a girl who found them. Over and over again the same kind of story is told. Two boys and a dog were chasing a rabbit. The rabbit disappeared under a pile of brush. The brush gave way under the boys' weight, and they tumbled through a shaft into the room of a cave. It sounds like *Alice in Wonderland,* doesn't it?

Sometimes it was a woodchuck that disappeared under a pile of rocks. Or a lost pig that was tracked to a hole in its pasture. A horse that stumbled into a hole in the ground led its rider to Lehman Caves in Nevada. A hunter, following a wounded bear into the side of a hill, found Mammoth Cave.

When it wasn't a rabbit or a woodchuck or a horse or a bear, it was a cow. For instance, a cow named Millicent always found her way to one special spot in the fields on hot summer days. Puzzled by the cow's behavior, her owner discovered that she was enjoying a cool breeze that came from a crack in the rocks. This crack led to the discovery of a vast cave below the ground. Millicent's cave is now known as Howe Caverns in New York, named after Lester Howe, the curious owner of the contented cow.

Many caves were first discovered by Indians and then rediscovered by white men. The Iroquois knew Howe Caverns as Otsgaragee, the "cave of the great galleries." Long before the days of Columbus, Mammoth Cave was used as a flint quarry and burial ground by the Indians.

The most exciting rediscovery of all was made by Jim White, a New Mexican cowboy who found a cave where the Basket Maker Indians had taken

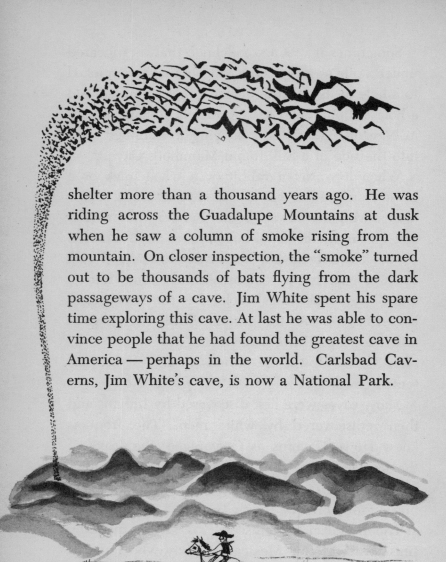

shelter more than a thousand years ago. He was riding across the Guadalupe Mountains at dusk when he saw a column of smoke rising from the mountain. On closer inspection, the "smoke" turned out to be thousands of bats flying from the dark passageways of a cave. Jim White spent his spare time exploring this cave. At last he was able to convince people that he had found the greatest cave in America — perhaps in the world. Carlsbad Caverns, Jim White's cave, is now a National Park.

Do you want to find a cave? You are not yet ready to be a cave detective, although you might want to become one some day. Right now, the best way for you to find a cave is to turn to page 121 at the back of this book and read the list of caves run by the National Park Service and by private individuals. There are more than a hundred of these, and at least one is likely to be within a day's drive of your home. The privately owned caves are called "commercial caves."

Mammoth Cave, in Kentucky, is the oldest commercial cave in the United States. It was opened to the public in 1816. The earliest guides were slaves who led parties of tourists through the cavern's twisting tunnels by lantern and candlelight. If you visited a cave in those days, you wore old clothes, because you had to climb over slippery rocks and crawl through mud and streams. To make sure you could find your way out again, you probably would have unrolled a ball of twine fastened to the opening of the cave.

Nowadays you can do your caving in ordinary clothes. The commercial cave owners, who call themselves the Cave Men of America, have installed electric lights and concrete footpaths, bridges and guardrails — and sometimes even elevators, motorboats, or tracks for "streetcars" that go uphill and down inside the cave! No one gets lost in a commercial cave. No one stubs his toe on a rock or bumps his head in a low tunnel. You can even dine in underground restaurants deep inside the cave.

Caves vary greatly, but every cave is interesting. Every cave gives you a chance to visit the strange world underneath the earth.

How do you enter a cave? Through a rabbit hole on the surface of the ground, or through an opening on the side of a rocky cliff?

If it's a rabbit hole, the door you use is actually a hole in the cave ceiling. Very often the rock roof of a cave has become so thin that it is readily broken or worn through. Sometimes a small hole is made — as small as a rabbit hole. Sometimes it is a very large one. Horses and tractors have been known to drop unexpectedly into caves that no one knew were there.

Commercial cave owners have enlarged the original entrances or have dug out new, more convenient front doors for visitors. Instead of wriggling through a hole and dropping down into the cave room, you descend by elevator, stairway, or winding ramp.

Hillside entrance to Mammoth Cave *(above)* was discovered by a hunter following a wounded bear. *(Below)* "Rabbit-hole" entrance to Crystal Cave, also in Kentucky.

If, however, you enter a cave through the side of a cliff, then the entrance may have been opened up during quarrying or road-building operations, or by a stream cutting a deeper and deeper valley. Most natural cave entrances are made in this way by streams.

Commercial owners have had to make fewer changes in the cliffside entrance than in the "rabbit hole." They leave the ferns that spring from cracks in the rock, and the trees that frame the cave's mouth. A door or a gate is enough to protect the cave's interior from thoughtless trespassers.

Once you are inside the cave, the temperature may surprise you. It varies only a degree or two the year round. In New England caves, the temperature averages 45 degrees; in Texas and Florida, it reaches almost 70 degrees. If you are caving in August, you will feel pleasantly cool under the ground, while in December the air will seem warm. Long before air-conditioning machinery was invented, air from Howe Caverns was forced aboveground to cool a hotel during the summer months.

It was once thought that such cool and even temperatures were good for people with lung diseases. In Mammoth Cave you can still see the

A cool cave looks cooler when its floor is smooth as ice.

remains of stone cottages once occupied by tubercular patients. These sunless underground hospitals were failures, of course; but for healthy people, cave air is refreshing. So breathe deeply as you follow your guide.

He will take you through long corridors which link together one hollowed-out room after another. You'll stop to stare at the stone sculpture that hangs from the ceiling and juts up from the floor. Stalactites, stalagmites, draperies of stone. Many of the passages wind through undecorated gray limestone. Flowstone and other formations, however, may be red, yellow, or earth brown. Pure calcite is creamy white, but there is little pure lime in the cave. Since the water may carry a good deal of iron for periods of many years, the "rust" — the red or brown deposit — may form colorful bands or layers. The water sometimes picks up traces of other minerals: copper or manganese, for example. Such mineral-laden water dyes the stone formations with soft colors as it builds them.

A few of the stalactites are dull-looking. These are "dead," because they are no longer touched by dripping water. The "live," growing stalactites are shiny, with a glistening surface that reflects the light from the overhead lamps.

The room in which you are standing may be called Aladdin's Palace, Fairies' Garden, or Solomon's Temple. Your guide points out rocks that look like Abraham Lincoln, the Capitol in Washington, and Mickey Mouse. Here's Elephant's Head. There's Pharaoh's Beard. Santa Claus is on the left and Huckleberry Finn up ahead.

This business of naming the cave formations is everybody's game. Depending on the kind of imagination that you have, you can see stalactite squash, stalagmite carrots, flowstone ham and eggs, sleeping lions and climbing lizards, or giants' teeth and angels' wings.

Some caves have a Wishing Well, a pool in which you can throw a penny as you make a wish. Almost every cave has a narrow, twisting passageway known as Fat Man's Misery, and many a cave has a Bridal Altar where marriages have actually been performed.

Cave guides like to tell the story of a fair maiden who was disappointed in love. Stamping her foot, she vowed, "I will never marry any man on the face of the earth." Then she fell in love and wanted to marry. To keep her vow, she married her beloved hundreds of feet under the earth, in one of the cave's shadowy rooms.

No two caves are alike. Some have little decora-

tion, but great canyonlike passages. The walls of others glitter with sparkling crystals or twisted milky-white helictites. Some caves display rare anthodites on the ceiling, gypsum flowers in narrow corridors, and cave pearls and coral-like formations in tiny pools.

In still other caves, immense galleries are crowded with massive structures of stone. The trail around Carlsbad's Big Room is a mile and a quarter long. In one spot the ceiling is 350 feet high. A thirty-story apartment house could be built there — with space for a baseball diamond and a tennis court.

In many caves, portions of the ceiling have collapsed. Enormous blocks of limestone and broken stalagmites that look like petrified logs litter the floors. A gigantic cave-in in Wyandotte Cave in Indiana built an underground mountain of rock fragments 175 feet high. When did this happen? A stalagmite on top of the rubble proves that the collapse occurred tens of thousands of years ago.

As you stop to look around, the guide points to

places in the rock where shells are visible. You can see cone-shaped shells and fan-shaped ones with scalloped edges in the ceilings of caves in Texas and Wisconsin. There are snail-like and clamlike shells in the walls of caves in Tennessee and Arkansas. There are spiral shells and tubes to be found in caves in South Dakota, Kentucky, and New York. All are silent witnesses to the days when ancient seas covered the land.

Sometimes on a cave tour, your guide may ask for silence. Then he flips a nearby switch, and the lights go out.

Everything is black. Jet black. Inky black. Not the darkness of outdoors at night when there is a faint glow from moon and stars or from a neighbor's house. Here in the cave is an absolute blackness — a dark which has never been pierced by sun or moon, and never will be.

Now you begin to hear sounds that you had not noticed before. The drip-drip-drip of water echoes through the room. There is a faint whir of wings as a bat flies overhead. The guide taps on hollow stalactites or folded stone draperies with a mallet, producing chimes or a simple tune.

Perhaps you remember reading about a man trapped in a tunnel. The story goes that he was startled by a hammering sound, until he realized that he was listening to his own heartbeats. You think of what it must be like to be lost in a cave with only a candle stub for company. Then the guide flips on the lights again, and the spell is broken.

A winding path takes you to lower and lower levels. Now the faint *ping* of dripping water is drowned out by the roar of an underground river.

51

Do all caves have rivers? No. In some, the water drained into a sunny valley long ago. In others, a stream appears briefly, only to disappear again through a crack in the wall or beneath a rock ledge.

But in Minnesota's Niagara Cave, Lost River plunges over a precipice to splash and echo on the rocks below — a waterfall 200 feet beneath the ground. In Mammoth and Howe Caverns, you can walk along the banks of the River Styx or cross an underground lake in a flat-bottomed boat. And if you visit Penn's Cave in Pennsylvania, your entire trip through the cave will be made by motorboat.

MAMMOTH CAVE, NATIONAL PARK SERVICE PHOTO

Traveling through a cave is like wandering through a giant anthill. The rooms are hollowed out helter-skelter. A twisting corridor may lead to an immense cathedral-like room, to a blank dead-end wall, or to a seemingly bottomless pit. If you were to make a map of the trail you have followed, you might find that you have been on several different levels. Some of the Kentucky caves have four and even five levels.

Small holes and deep pits along the way hint of unexplored passages. But you can't go exploring here. As a matter of fact, you have looped back to the doorway through which you entered. Above the ground the sun is shining. You blink your eyes until you grow accustomed to its brightness.

Chapter 5

Kinds of Caves

A GEOLOGIST WOULD SAY that the caves you have been reading about until now are *solution caves*. They have been hollowed out of limestone, because limestone is the commonest rock that can be dissolved or "eaten away." There are also gypsum and marble caverns that are formed in exactly the same way. It's the old, old story of acid rain water and underground streams and stalactites and flowstone draperies. Still other caves may be carved by pounding waves and rushing streams, by wind and rain and frost, or by the special work of earthquakes and volcanoes. They may occur in any kind of rock, from hard, hard granite to soft sandstone.

Sea Caves

Take sea caves, for instance. Hundreds of thousands of years ago a sudden movement of the earth's crust caused a crack in the cliffs that lined a shore. Pounding waves enlarged the crack, making it deeper, wider, higher, until the crack became a

hole, and the hole became a cave. The hard rock of the cliff was not dissolved by the ocean's waves. It was gouged out, ground down, by the abrasive action of the sea.

You understand "abrasive action" whenever it's your turn to wash dishes, whenever you clean a greasy frying pan. First you fill it with hot water and detergent and put it aside to soak. When you pour off the water, most of the grease has disappeared. It dissolved in the hot water.

But alas, your work is not yet finished. There are still sticky spots on the bottom of the pan. You attack them with steel wool, rubbing and scrubbing until you've worn them away. When you rinse the pan now, it's shiny clean. It has been cleaned by the dissolving action of the hot water and the abrasive action of the steel wool, with power provided by you.

The sea provides the power that scoops out the cave, but it is the broken bits of rock, fragments that have been ground down to pebbles and fine sand, that are the real destructive force. They work like steel wool, or the sandpaper that you use to smooth rough wood. They work slowly, but given time enough, they wear away the rock. Another word for this slow wearing away is "erosion."

The largest American sea cave — an opening 1,500 feet long and 100 feet high — is on the coast of Oregon. It was discovered in 1880 by a sailor who rowed into the cave in a small boat. Marooned there by a storm, he found that the cave was occupied by sea lions.

Nowadays visitors enter Sea Lion Caves from the top of the cliff, traveling downward by stairway and ramp. The ocean entrance of the cave is under water except at low tide, but from the rear of the big room you can still watch the sea lions. There are hundreds of these slippery, shiny creatures — frisky young pups and 2,000-pound bulls — flopping over the rocks and waving their flippers as they swim. Above their heads, in crevices on the rough walls, flocks of web-footed sea birds make their nests each summer.

Smaller sea caves are scattered up and down the Pacific and Atlantic coasts and along the shores of the Great Lakes. At La Jolla, California, tourists can see fossilized shells in the rock, and eels and octopuses in the water that covers a cave floor. Anemone Cave, on the coast of Maine, shelters starfish, sea urchins, sponges, and the sea anemones for which the cave is named.

If you visit Anemone Cave, be sure to look for Thunder Hole, a small cave about a mile away. At high tide, waves strike against the cave's rear wall and bounce upward, making their way out through a slot in the roof. The spurting spray looks like a geyser or the spout of a whale. *Blowholes* like this one are often found in sea caves.

Most sea caves are not very big, and the entrance is likely to be flooded at high tide. Usually such a cave is just one room, with walls stained green, pink, or purple by minerals in the rock and in the seaweed which grows in the shallow water. No stalactites, no stalagmites, no flowstone draperies. But some sea caves are very beautiful. Perhaps you've heard of the Blue Grotto of Capri in Italy. Sunlight reflected through the water from the cave's narrow mouth bathes the sea-carved room in a sapphire-blue light. ("Grotto," by the way, is still another word for "cave" — used more often by poets than by scientists.)

Fingal's Cave, in the Scottish Hebrides, is almost as well known as the Blue Grotto. During stormy periods in Scottish history, it served as a harbor for pirates and smugglers. When Felix Mendelssohn, the great composer of music, toured the Hebrides, he was so moved by the cave's wild beauty that he wrote an overture named "Fingal's Cave."

Canyon Caves

It's hard to imagine land much drier than the canyon country of the American Southwest. Only seven inches of rain fall each year in Arizona, compared with thirty to forty inches in most states. Yet even in this dry country, water has eaten away the land, carving narrow valleys and flat-topped hills — and caves of a special sort.

Swift-flowing rivers carrying pebbles and gravel traveled down from the Rockies. Sluggish streams fed by sudden summer cloudbursts became roaring torrents. Together they cut through the soft sandstone. They scooped out the rock, digging caves at the base of the cliffs. Over the years, the valleys grew deeper, the stream beds lower, until the caves were left high and dry on the canyon walls.

Canyon caves bear little resemblance to the dark limestone caverns. The shallow rooms are only partly shaded from the sunlight. The walls have been worn smooth by wind and fine sand, and the cave floor is littered with blocks of stone that have fallen from the roof. From a distance, the caves look like balconies that have been cut into the sides of the cliff. Since no mineral-bearing waters sink down through the rock, there are no decorations, no formations.

No one has yet explored all of the Southwest's canyon caves, but many of them are now part of the National Park System. If you are lucky enough to make a trip to this part of the country, perhaps you can visit Mesa Verde National Park in Colorado, or one of the many National Monuments in Arizona. Here you will find dozens of examples of the open canyon caves. Early Indians used some of these

The Indians of the Southwest built houses in canyon caves.

MESA VERDE, NATIONAL PARK SERVICE PHOTOS

Below: A large open canyon cave shelters the remains of a group of Indian dwellings.

caves for temporary shelter and occupied others for hundreds of years.

Lava Caves

There's one kind of cave where water plays no part. That's the *lava cave*.

Deep inside this shrinking, cracking, quaking earth of ours, there are pockets of hot melted rock. Not solid hard rock, but thick doughy stuff that pushes its way upward until it reaches the surface of the earth. The melted rock — lava — may burst through the ground under tremendous pressure, so that it breaks into tiny fragments as it cools. Or it may slowly ooze out of cracks, forming a river of liquid rock.

The lava river flows across the plains and winds through the valleys, often as fast as five miles an hour. When it meets the air and the ground, it cools and hardens in much the same way that hot fudge sauce does when you pour it on cold ice cream. But the outer surface of the lava cools first, while the fiery interior continues to flow. Underneath, as the liquid rock drains away, there is only an empty tunnel. In fact, a lava cave.

Some lava caves are narrow tubes, too small for

people to climb through. Others are mile-long passages with high arched roofs, larger than the man-made tunnels under the Hudson River in New York. The rippled floors, marked by the passage of the fiery streams, still seem to be in motion. And the ceilings have produced dripping stalactites.

There are lava caves in most of the western states. There are nearly 300 in California alone, and about twenty are open to public visits. There are also several long spectacular lava caves in Hawaii.

LAVA BEDS, NATIONAL PARK SERVICE PHOTO BY JACK E. BOUCHER

CAPTAIN JACK'S CAVE

Ice Caves

From hot lava rivers to perpetual ice seems like a big jump. But some lava caves contain blocks of ice that never melt. Above the cave, the sun beats down until it is so hot that the thermometer reads 115 degrees. Scraggly cedar trees that have found a foothold in the barren rock offer no shade. Only twenty feet below the ground, however, you can redden your nose and freeze your toes as you walk over frozen floors and chip icicles from the ceiling. Not icicles of stone, but real icicles of frozen water. In one cave in New Mexico there is a wall of blue-green ice that's fifty feet wide, fourteen feet high, and no one knows how thick.

"But, but —" you interrupt, " how can there be ice when the thermometer reads 115 degrees?"

Even in New Mexico, temperatures drop below freezing during the winter. Cold surface air sinks slowly into the lava rock, chilling it many feet below the ground. Once the porous stone is thoroughly chilled, it stores up the cold for a long time. When melting snows and spring rains bring water into the cave, the water freezes. The bed of ice thickens. The cave remains cold, no matter what the temperature is like at the surface of the ground.

How old is the ice in these caves? Indians melted it for drinking water in this land of few surface streams and little rain. Early white settlers cut it into blocks, using it to preserve their meat in summer. But no matter how much ice was removed from the cave, more continued to form. Some scientists think that there may have been ice in the lava caves long before men lived in North America.

These desert iceboxes (which you can see in New Mexico and Arizona, as well as in the commercial lava caves) are not the only kind of ice cave. In the Rocky Mountains and in Mount Rainier National Park, there are glacial caves. They are hollowed out of ice rather than rock. They form not when water freezes, but when it melts.

If you have ever dug into a snowbank until you built a burrow large enough to hide in, you'll have some idea of what glacial caves are like. The walls, the floors, the ceilings, are of ice. They change in size and shape each year, enlarging in summer as warm air melts back the walls and becoming smaller in winter. Streams of water from melting ice flow through the tunnels, scalloping the walls and spreading gravel over the frozen floors. By fall, slabs of ice drop from the ceiling at the slightest vibration, and ice boulders weighing many tons

block the passageways. Tourists may travel to the entrance of Mount Rainier's ice caves, but the caves themselves are too dangerous to explore.

There are ice caverns, too, in New England and sometimes as far south as Kentucky. When the snow melts in the spring, it trickles down to the underground rooms and there freezes, remaining frozen until August or September. But for really big ice caverns you would have to climb high up in the mountains of Europe or Asia. Here ice fills the limestone rooms, forming frozen waterfalls and huge underground skating rinks. Cold winds moan through the passageways, and dampened clothing freezes almost instantly. There are giant icicles hanging from the ceilings and thick columns of milky-white ice rising from the floors. In the high Himalaya Mountains of Asia, a pillar of perpetual ice is a shrine sacred to a Hindu god. Thousands of pilgrims travel over the mountain trails each summer to worship at its base.

It would be nice to say that there are four kinds of caves, or five. Something definite like the number of ounces in a pound or feet in a yard. But kinds of caves aren't as easy to count as ounces or feet. Openings in the ground can have many different causes, and the cave nearest your home may not be like any of those already described.

Fault Caves

Perhaps you have visited a fault cave. Caves of this kind are formed suddenly when the earth's crust pushes upward and squeezes sideways until great cracks, known as *faults,* appear in the rocks. Fault caves are seldom more than narrow tunnels and small straight-sided rooms. Unless running water has found its way into their passages, they probably look today much as they did millions of years ago.

Boulder Caves

Perhaps the cave you know best was created during the Ice Age, when water froze and melted at the edge of the glaciers, and frost action split off great chunks of rock. Hollow spaces were left behind or beneath these rocks. As the glaciers melted, streams enlarged the openings and polished the broken rocks, often carving them into strange shapes. These caves are known as *boulder* or *split-rock caves*. Polar Caves and Lost River Caves in New Hampshire had their beginnings when slow-moving icecaps covered the White Mountains.

Man-made Caves

Perhaps you have seen a man-made cave dug by miners hunting for copper or salt or by masons quarrying stone. In many parts of the country there are caves like these. They are sometimes used for storing surplus grain and butter or even important documents. Enormous man-made caves house ships and planes, factories and hospitals. But that is another story.

Chapter 6

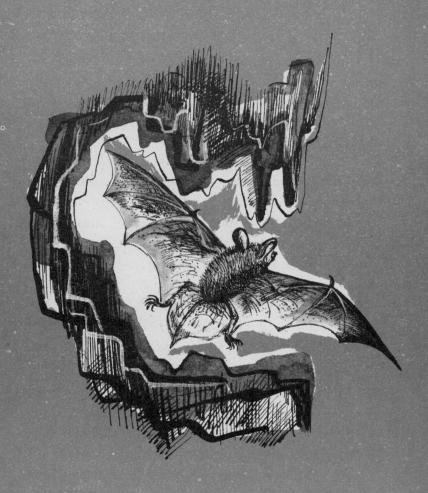

Cave Animals

Cave Animals

Perhaps you think of a cave as just a cave — a dark, damp underground room. But a scientist would tell you that under the one rock roof there are really three separate zones, like three apartments.

1. First there's the entranceway, often well lighted.
2. Then there's the twilight zone, into which some light penetrates.
3. Far back in the cave is the inky-black interior.

Each of these apartments has its own set of tenants. Tenants in apartment 1 seldom meet their neighbors in apartment 3.

The entrance of the cave seems more like a hotel than an apartment house. Animals come and go. Some are summer visitors, taking shelter in the cave until their children are full grown. Others are winter vacationers, looking for a place where they can take a long quiet snooze until spring.

Owls and phoebes build their nests here. Foxes, skunks, and woodchucks use it as a den in which to raise their families. Raccoons and snakes sometimes hibernate here. So do mosquitoes and some kinds of moths and flies. But none of these animals really needs the cave apartment. If any of them can't find a cave, they'll settle for a rock crevice or a hollow log or a burrow under the ground.

In apartment 2 you'll meet the commuters — animals who spend most of their lives in caves, but who travel outside to find their food.

On a lime-coated ledge, you may see a pile of shredded bark. It's the nest of a cave rat. The rat will eat anything from seeds and nuts to the remains of a ham sandwich. When it's not eating, it's collecting odd bits of trash — pebbles and pennies, cigarettes and bottle caps — and storing them in its nest. In the West, these bright-eyed collectors are called "pack rats."

The best known of the cave commuters is the bat. Best known and most misunderstood.

Bats *don't* get tangled in girls' hair. Ever.

Bats *don't* drink human blood — bats in the United States, that is. (There are vampire bats in Mexico and South America that live on the blood of birds and mammals, and occasionally of humans.)

Bats *don't* bite except to protect themselves. What's more, some naturalists have kept bats and have taught them to take meal worms from tweezers and to drink water from an eye dropper.

What about bats that carry rabies? Like dogs, foxes, skunks, and other mammals, bats *may* carry the virus of this serious disease. But only rarely. Possibly one in a million of our insect-eating bats may carry rabies.

Bats are *not* blind. Their eyes are not much bigger than pencil points, but they work perfectly well both in daylight and in the perpetual twilight of the cave apartment.

When bats fly at night in total darkness, ducking under stalactites, circling around pillars, dodging through narrow passages, they depend on their ears rather than their eyes to guide them. Bats send out sound waves — noises too high-pitched for human ears to catch. These squeaks bounce back from cave

Millions of bats fly in and out of Carlsbad Caverns daily.

walls and formations, warning the bats of obstacles in the way.

The scientist who discovered this remarkable feature of bat hearing named it *echo-location*. During World War II he taught blinded soldiers to use echo-location to find their way in unfamiliar places.

Sonar works in the same way. Men send down sounds through the water. The sound, bouncing back from the ocean bottom, tells them how deep the water is.

Bats don't . . . Bats are not . . . What *are* bats, anyway?

Bats are furry, warm-blooded creatures who nurse their young with milk. They are the only flying mammals. (Flying squirrels don't really fly. They just glide from tree to tree.)

Not all bats live in caves. In summer, some roost in trees or dark attics or church belfries. (You've heard of bats in the belfry!) Some fly south in the winter, while others spend the cold months hibernating underground in mines or in crevices in the rocks, as well as in caves. They have a homing instinct, which brings them back to the same cave or other roost year after year.

Winter and summer, most cave bats are social creatures, living side by side on the walls and ceiling of their dark apartment. Their tiny claws grasp

74

rough spots on the rock, and they hang head down, with folded wings — male bats, female bats, baby bats clinging to their mothers, packed as close together as sardines in a can. In one square foot of cave wall space, there are often 300 bats. More than eight million bats spend their summer days in a remote section of Carlsbad Caverns, while in Ney Cave in Texas the bat colony was once estimated at between twenty and thirty million!

75

When millions of these animals live in one cave, their droppings, known as *guano*, form deep deposits that are rich in minerals. Saltpeter obtained from bat guano was formerly used in the production of gunpowder. Mammoth Cave bats supplied gunpowder that helped defeat the British in the Battle of New Orleans in 1815, and bats south of the Mason-Dixon line were on the side of the Confederacy during the Civil War. Today the Atomic Energy Commission is using bats to study the effect of atomic radiation.

These timid creatures of the night also work for peace. Bat guano is as good for fertilizer as it is for gunpowder. Long before commercial caves were equipped with electric lights, cave owners were mining guano and selling it to farmers. There was a time when finding a guano cave was as profitable as discovering gold. Carlsbad Caverns alone have provided more than 100,000 tons of bat-made fertilizer.

Bats are great insect eaters. One bat will eat half its weight in insects in a single night. Imagine how many insects are destroyed by a million bats!

In Texas, huge wooden bat roosts were built in the hope that colonies of bats would occupy the towers and devour mosquitoes, which were transmitting yellow fever.

In summer in the South, bats sleep in their cave apartments throughout the day. Farther north, they may hang in barns and lofts. Just before sunset they begin to stir. There's a whispering, fluttering noise as wings unfold. It grows in volume, becoming a swish, a rush, a roar. Hundreds, thousands, millions of bats spiral upward from the cave's mouth, darkening the sky and then swooping down to drink and eat. At dawn they return home, wheeling down and flying back into the cave at a terrific rate of speed.

On midsummer evenings it takes four hours for Carlsbad's bat colony to clear the mouth of the cave. Tourists gather at the entrance to watch the spectacular flight. By the time the bats return, they have eaten more than eleven tons of moths, flies, beetles, and mosquitoes.

In fall, as the insect population disappears, most of Carlsbad's bats fly south. But in many northern states, bats move into caves for a long winter's sleep. They hang motionless from the walls, their body processes slowed down until they are scarcely breathing. In March or April they venture outdoors again.

Most of what is known about bats has been

learned only in the last thirty years, when a few scientists started bat-banding. More than 100,000 bats have been marked with tiny aluminum bands, which are fastened around their forearms. Each band has a number stamped on it, as if it were an automobile license plate. A record of the number and when and where the bat was tagged is kept by the United States Fish and Wildlife Service. Anyone finding a banded bat is asked to report the number to the Fish and Wildlife Service.

In this way many people help keep track of bat comings and goings. A bat banded in 1939, for instance, was found again in 1963, proving that bats can live as long as twenty-four years. Another banded bat migrated 810 miles from Carlsbad Caverns to Mexico, while a third traveled from Minnesota to Wisconsin in order to return to its home cave.

Bats are dwellers in the twilight zone of the cave, but who lives in the zone of total darkness?

Far back in apartment 3 are animals that never see the light. They are born underground. They live and die there, just as their parents, their grandparents, and a long line of ancestors have done. They are year-round, lifelong cave animals, most of whom could not survive for long outside their pitch-black world.

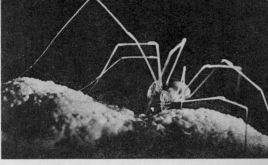

Animals living in the total darkness of caves lose their sight. *Right:* Blind spider.

Blind salamander. The eyelids of its unused eyes grow together after it was born.

Blind crayfish carrying eggs. Notice that all these unseen creatures have no color.

Blind fish. It seems to find its food by "feeling" when the water nearby is disturbed.

These perpetual cave dwellers have several things in common. They are white or pale pink in color. They are blind. To make up for their lack of sight, they have sharpened senses of smell and touch. Depending on the kinds of animals they are, they have overgrown feelers, sensitive skins, or fine body hairs to help them in their lifelong game of blind man's buff.

The best known of these dark-adapted cave animals are the blind fish. They are from two to four inches long, with pale, transparent skins through which their blood vessels can be seen. Blind fish begin to develop eyes before they are born. But their eyes never develop fully. Adult blind fish have only fatty bulges where their eyes once were.

Blind salamanders are found in underground waterways in Missouri, Texas, and the Southeast. The Missouri salamander can see when it is born, but its eyelids grow together as it becomes adult. Its Texas cousin is startlingly beautiful, with a shiny white body and feathery gills. The tiny eyes are completely covered with skin.

The list of pale, blind animals living in caves is a long one. There are pearly-white crayfish, cousins of the brown "crawdads" of our brooks, with long slender feelers to help them find food. In a few caves, shrimp have been found. They are so transparent that they are almost invisible. The shallow water in one Oklahoma cave looked as if someone had stirred a bottle of cream into it. But the "cream" was made up of thousands of blind white water bugs and flatworms. The flatworms, related to tapeworms and hookworms, are delicate little animals. They shrivel up and die if they are exposed to sunlight for even a few minutes.

Close by the water are other ghost creatures — pale, long-legged crickets; blind, wingless beetles, whose bodies are covered with sensitive hairs; white pill bugs; and tiny blind spiders.

What do these animals of perpetual darkness live on? Each other, of course. The smallest of them feed on bat guano, mushrooms, and decaying leaves and bits of wood that are washed into the cave. The middle-sized creatures eat the little animals, and the biggest ones feast on anything they can catch. Water fleas eat dead beetles. Flatworms eat water fleas. And blind fish eat flatworms. It's an endless chain.

These cave creatures have long been of interest to scientists. Are they blind because they have lived in darkness for so many generations? Did their eyes gradually grow smaller, or become covered with skin, or disappear entirely because there was no need for them?

Experiments with a blind salamander have shown that when it is exposed to certain kinds of light, its eyes begin to grow. By the time the animal is five years old, it can see, even though its ancestors have been dark-adapted for centuries.

Scientists have also wondered why cave life has not produced phosphorescent animals with bodies that glow in the dark, the way that fireflies and some deep-sea animals do. There *are* some phosphorescent cave animals. For example, in Waitomo Cave in New Zealand, thousands of tiny "caterpillars" hang from the ceiling of the cavern. Twinkling like stars, they give off an eerie blue light. The light attracts flying insects on which the caterpillars feed. These "glowworms" are extremely sensitive to sound. When there's the slightest noise in the cave, it means "Lights out!"

Cave Plants

Unlike animals, green plants cannot become adapted to the dark. They depend on light in order to make their food. Acorns brought in by pack rats or orange pits dropped by tourists occasionally

sprout in dark cave rooms. Thin and pale, they grow for a few days, until the food supply stored in the seed is used up. Then they topple over and die.

There are a few plants that aren't green and so do not need light. Among these are mushrooms. A cave's moist air and even temperature provide the kind of home that mushrooms thrive in. They live on guano or decaying wood. In Europe, people often visit caves in order to gather mushrooms. In the United States, most commercial mushroom farmers plant their crops in underground rooms.

If this book had been written fifty years ago, the report on underground gardens would have stopped right here. But now green plants, such as mosses

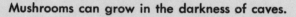

Mushrooms can grow in the darkness of caves.

CHARLES E. MOHR PHOTO

and ferns, grow in caves. Can you guess what has made the difference?

Electricity, of course. Where cave owners have installed electric lights, green plants may cling to stalactites and turn gray stone walls green.

But the same electric lights that make plant life possible have lessened your chances of seeing cave animals. Bats still roost occasionally in commercial caves; but the blind fish, crayfish, and salamanders have hidden away — far from the lights and the sound of tramping feet.

Chapter 7

Cave Men

CLOUDS OF DUST drift from the mouth of the cave. Inside are strange-looking people wearing goggles and masks — dust-covered men armed with picks and shovels, dust-covered women with trowels and sieves. What are they doing — kneeling, bending, crawling across the cave floor?

Suddenly one man holds up something in his hand. The others drop their tools and hurry to his side. He is holding a pointed piece of stone. With loving care, he carries it to a box just outside the cave. There are other things in the box too — an eyeless, grinning skull; a broken jar.

What's going on here? Have we stumbled across a lost tribe of cave men?

These people are *archaeologists,* scientists who study the lives of prehistoric men. They wear goggles and masks to protect themselves from the blinding, choking dust that rises from the cave floor as they dig. What are they looking for? Buried treasure? Yes, of a special kind. Not gold nor jewels, but dusty bones, jagged bits of stone, and fragments

of clay. If they are lucky, what they find will tell them about how men lived in prehistoric times.

"Prehistoric" means "before history." *History* starts with the first people to leave written records of their lives, the Babylonians and the Egyptians. History begins six thousand years ago. But when does *prehistory* begin? Four billion years ago, when the earth was formed? Or two hundred million years ago, when dinosaurs devoured the huge leaves of the giant tree ferns? You might say that the pre-history of man begins one or two million years ago, when the earliest men that we know about lived. And it's only in the last hundred years or so that there has been any serious study of prehistory. So there are many gaps in the story of man that archaeologists have not yet been able to fill in.

Clues to the story of prehistoric man are buried in caves all over the world. One of the earliest chapters has been found in China, in the Choukoutien[1] Caves, near the city of Peiping. Men and women lived at the mouth of these limestone caverns half a million years ago, during the early part of the Ice Age. Although the brains of these prehistoric men were one fourth smaller than the brains of modern men, these ancient people were real men — not man-apes nor ape-men. They were a tribe of hunters; they feasted on deer meat, varying their diet with steak of the giant mammoth and roast leg of camel. And sometimes with the flesh of other human beings! They chipped stones to make hammers and crude knives, and on the floor of the cave they built clay hearths and kindled fires.

How do archaeologists know all this? The cave men couldn't write. They couldn't even speak in

[1] Say: JOE-KOE-TYEN.

the way that we understand speech today. How were they able to leave records that would last for 500,000 years?

In place of written records, they left the bones of the animals they hunted and the stone tools used to kill and clean them. In place of written records, they left bits of charred wood, charcoal, and ashes from the first fires kindled by man's hand. In place of written records, they left — themselves. Their skulls and teeth, their jaws and thigh bones.

The cave men left these records, and the cave preserved them. Century after century, water trickled down the walls and dripped from the cave ceilings until the bones and tools and bits of wood were coated with lime. As the lime hardened into stone, they became a part of the cave itself, preserved until archaeologists came along with drills and saws and cut them loose.

The record of early man stops with the people of the Choukoutien Caves and isn't continued again for a long time. Not for 400,000 years!

This doesn't mean that there were no men living and hunting and exploring their world during all those centuries. They were there, all right, but most of them lived in camps in the open instead of in caves, and the records they left behind have been destroyed. There are traces of other early men in Africa and in the Near East, and future digging will doubtless uncover many more. But the next complete chapter in this story of man begins in the caves of western Europe.

These caves, particularly in France and Spain, are real treasure-troves for the archaeologists. They are chock full of records, arranged in such neat order that the prehistorian can read straight through them, from 100,000 B.C. almost down to modern times.

If you're wondering how it's possible to do this, think back to the rainy afternoon when you cleaned off the shelves in your room. Your stamp album and the box of writing paper that Aunt Mary gave you for Christmas were on top. Then came a souvenir from your vacation trip, a Monopoly game, a spelling test that you got an "A" on last year. Underneath these there was a diary kept for two weeks, a picture of your brother when he was a baby; and way down on the bottom of the pile, a battered box of crayons that you used in the second grade.

There's a story here about you. But you have to read it backward, starting with the stamp album

ROOF OF CAVE

MOUTH OF CAVE

WALL OF CAVE

PRESENT CAVE FLOOR

ORIGINAL CAVE FLOOR

Pottery

Later Man

Stone Tool

Extinct Mammals

Bones of Early Man

Fire

that you still use and working down to your old crayons. And that's the way archaeologists read the stories they find in caves.

Fortunately for the prehistorians, the people who lived in caves were not very tidy housekeepers. They left the remains of their meals, their tools, even their dead, on the rough stone floor. Mud was washed in. Lime-charged water dripped from the ceiling. Each year the layers of debris became thicker and thicker.

When the weather grew warmer or the game they hunted scarcer, the cave dwellers moved away. Animals moved in — huge cave bears, hyenas, animals unlike any that live today. Their bones formed another layer on the cave floor.

As time went on, the climate changed, and people came back to the cave. Different people who left different tools — bone needles and fishhooks and spear throwers. They also left garbage — the bones of mammoth and reindeer and bison. New layers were piled on top of the old ones. This went on for tens of thousands of years.

If you could cut straight through the pile of debris in one of these caves, it would look like a giant seven-layer cake. Layer after layer separated by clay and gravel and limestone. On the bottom of the pile is the story of the first people who lived in the cave — low-browed, stoop-shouldered men and women whose tools weren't much better than those in the Choukoutien Caves. Then came more modern-looking people, who buried their dead and decorated them with shell beads and red coloring matter. And so up and up, until in the topmost layer just under the cave ceiling, there are iron tools and glazed pottery jars.

Who discovered America? Why, Columbus, of course, in 1492. Or Leif Ericson in the year 1000.

That's not what the story of prehistory says. According to archaeologists, people were living in

North America 30,000 years before Columbus first set sail. Who were these people?

While cave men were chasing reindeer herds in the valleys of France, bands of Asian hunters traveled across the narrow neck of land which then connected Siberia and Alaska. Game was plentiful on the new continent, and the first hunters were followed by others. Slowly these immigrants from Asia wandered through the forests and along the rivers of North America. Slowly they traveled south to the very tip of South America. In a cave in Chile, archaeologists have found charred bits of wood and dusty bones that are more than 8,000 years old.

Who were these men and women who discovered America? Who were these people whose descendants Columbus called "Indians"? Prehistorians do not even know what the first settlers looked like, but they are sure of their existence because of records found in caves. In Sandia Cave in New Mexico, there are mammoth tusks and charred bits of camel jaws in the same layer with dart points and stone knives that could have been made only by human hands. In Gypsum Cave in Nevada, the curved claws and woolly red hairs of giant sloths, extinct for 10,000 years, have been found lying *above* stone tools and remains of ancient fires.

A mammoth skull with tusks in a museum, showing height

Jaw of a prehistoric camel

Stone knives found in New Mexico

Prehistoric ears of corn of different sizes

And in Bat Cave in New Mexico, archaeologists have dug up tiny ears of corn no bigger than your little finger — the grandparent of today's corn on the cob.

One of the richest chapters in American prehistory was uncovered in the Four Corners region, where New Mexico, Arizona, Utah, and Colorado meet. Here archaeologists have found records of hunters and farmers who stored their food and buried their dead in the shallow sandstone caves of the Southwest. These early Americans left their signatures behind them in the form of woven reed baskets with striking colorful designs, and so have become known as the Basket Makers.

In most limestone caverns only the hardest substances — stone and bone — can resist the dampness. But the hot, dry air of the canyon caves has preserved the remains of the Basket Makers. It has turned them into mummies whose hair, skin, clothing, and facial expressions are still recognizable.

Archaeologists can tell you all about Basket Maker families — how the babies slept on woven cradle boards, under fur blankets made of rabbit skins; how the women wore their hair short, chopped off just below the ears with stone knives. Twisted strands of hair made the best basket handles and the best rope, and yards of hair twine have been dug out of storage pits in the cave floor. *Women's* hair, that is. The men wore their hair long, with side loops and bouncing braids in back!

They can even describe the Basket Maker dogs, which were sometimes given formal burial with their favorite bones placed at their sides. Mummies of two prehistoric dogs, found in Arizona and exhibited at a Boston dog show, won blue ribbons as the oldest dogs in the show.

Above the remains of the earliest Basket Makers

Above: Basket found in cave shows colorful woven design.

Left: Striped bag is woven of fibers of the yucca plant.

there are later records. Clothing and hair styles change. Baskets gradually give way to pottery, crude clay bowls at first, and then elaborately painted and carefully shaped jars. There are turkey-feather blankets and woven cotton cloth.

The caves where the Basket Makers lived are divided into circular rooms with mud walls and log roofs. Rough stone walls come next, and finally cut stone blocks are laid one above the other until walls and towers reach to the ceilings of the caves.

When Leif Ericson was sailing along the shores of Vinland, when he was "discovering" America, the descendants of the Basket Makers were building seven-story apartment houses on top of the cliffs and in the caves of the Southwest. (If you think that seven stories isn't so high, remember that New York's first seven-story building wasn't put up until 1869, and then it was considered a remarkable achievement.) The builders of these cave sky-scrapers are known as Pueblos, a name that Spanish explorers gave to both the people and their villages.

The peaceful Pueblo farmers, who were in constant danger of raids from wandering tribes, found their cliff dwellings easy to defend. When enemies threatened, they climbed ladders to their fortress homes and pulled their stairways up after them. Their cave cities often housed hundreds of families. Cliff Palace in Mesa Verde National Park in Colorado was an eight-story structure with more than 200 rooms. Keet Seel and Betatakin (which means Hillside House) in Navajo National Monument in Arizona contained more than 150 rooms each. Archaeologists have found thousands of these cave apartment houses in the Four Corners region.

The cliff dwellers were the last cave men of the Southwest. A terrible drought 200 years before the voyages of Columbus drove the Pueblos from their canyon homes and valley farms to more fertile lands.

Some of their descendants are still living today on reservations in New Mexico and Arizona.

In caves and rock shelters all over the United States, there are other stories of prehistoric animals and men. Mastodon bones have been dug up in caves in Maryland. Indians mined flint in Mammoth Cave, leaving behind ladders and bark torches and turkey-feather fans. As far back as 1813, a mummy of a woman dressed in deerskins was placed on exhibition in Mammoth Cave. Another Mammoth mummy was uncovered in 1935. There are

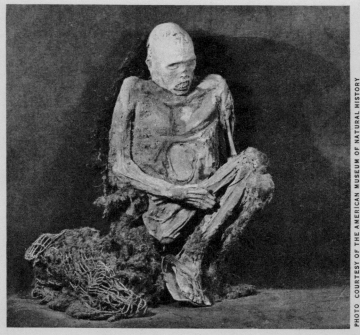

Basket Maker remains in Texas, and moccasin tracks hardened in the clay of Wyandotte Cave in Indiana. Arrow points have been found in Pennsylvania, and pottery jars in New York caves.

Perhaps the most exciting of all cave discoveries was made, not by an archaeologist, but by a five-year-old girl. It happened in northern Spain, in 1879, in the Cave of Altamira. Maria, daughter of Don Marcellino de Sautuola,[1] was keeping her father company while he sifted through dirt on the cave floor in search of Ice Age tools. Growing restless, she waved her candle about and wished that she had a better place to play than in the dark, low-ceilinged passageways.

Suddenly she shrieked, *"Toros! Toros!"*

Don Marcellino was bewildered. *"Toros"* is the Spanish word for "bulls," and of course there were no bulls in the cave. He stared at his daughter's pointing finger, and then he too felt like crying out in wonder.

On the uneven rock ceiling over his head there was a procession of animals. A leaping wild horse, a galloping boar, a graceful deer, and horned bison

[1] Say: sow-too-OH-lah.

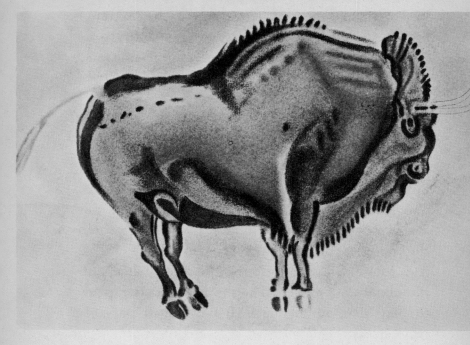

Painting of a bull in the Cave of Altamira, Spain

that Maria had mistaken for bulls. These were prehistoric paintings, pictures fully as old as the dart
points and scrapers buried under the cave floor.
Not crude scrawls either, but beautifully drawn,
richly colored pictures — as good as any done in
modern times.

As good as any done in modern times — that was
the trouble. These pictures were *too* good. No one

would believe Don Marcellino. Everyone was sure that he had hired an artist to decorate his cave. Peasants in the village, professors in Madrid, archaeologists of France and Germany and the United States, all cried, "Forgery! Fake! For shame!"

Don Marcellino died, and Maria was a grown woman before paintings were found in other caves. Then the learned world admitted its mistake, and shamefaced archaeologists made pilgrimages to Altamira to see the ancient art gallery.

In the years that followed, paintings were found in more than a hundred caves in France and Spain. Almost all of the ancient animal kingdom is represented on the walls and ceilings of these underground rooms. These are paintings of mammoths and reindeer, lions and bears, rhinoceroses and wolves, birds and fish and shaggy ponies, as well as occasional pictures of men. There's sculpture in the caves, too: clay figures of cave bears and bison and horses carved on reindeer horns.

As recently as 1940, four French schoolboys decided to explore a hole at the base of an uprooted tree. The hole was only three feet deep, but at its bottom was a narrower, longer shaft. The boys slid down, to discover what has become one of the most famous caves in the world: the Lascaux[1] Cave. It

[1] Say: lah-SKOE.

contains larger than life-size pictures of a whole prehistoric zoo.

For a time, Lascaux Cave was operated as a commercial cave. But the paintings which had lasted for so many centuries were threatened by the moist air currents and what they carried in from outside. To keep these priceless ancient art from being covered, and perhaps destroyed, the cave has been closed to the public.

How and why were these pictures painted on the walls of caves? The "how" is easy to answer. The reds and browns, the yellows and violets and blacks, were mineral colors, found in the clay and rock of the caves. When men ground them up and mixed them with animal fat, they became paint. Sometimes the outlines of the figures were scratched into the stone with sharp tools. Sometimes they were painted on the surface with brushes of feathers or animal hairs or the frayed ends of twigs. Sometimes the paint was blown on the moist stone through hollow bones.

When the artist's work was done, the even temperature and damp, still air of the cave preserved it.

Many of the pictures are covered with a transparent layer of lime. In others, the paint is fresh and wet — after 15,000 years!

But why? All of the pictures were drawn in rear rooms and dark passageways, in the remotest, blackest places in the caves. Clearly they were not painted just because they were nice to look at, as are the pictures that we hang on our walls today.

Most archaeologists think that the cave paintings were meant to be magic. If you've ever wished on a chicken bone or knocked on wood for luck, you've tried magic too. But the cave men's magic was deadly serious. If it didn't work, the whole tribe might starve. Or at least that's the way they figured it.

A painting of a reindeer whose skin was pierced by darts, or of a mammoth with a big arrowhead painted on it, was supposed to bring luck to the hunters. The more plentiful the pictures, the more plentiful the food. Or at least that is the way it seemed to them.

Although the cave paintings of western Europe are the best known, they are far from the only ones that have been discovered. Cave art galleries in South Africa shelter lively hunting scenes and sprightly dancers, as well as portraits of the giraffes and elands, the hippopotamuses and ostriches that roamed the plains or hid in the steaming jungles of long ago. These surprisingly modern-looking paintings were done by ancestors of the Bushmen more than 10,000 years ago.

In many places in North America, from Canada to Texas, from California to Ohio, caves and boulders are decorated with Indian pictures. The Basket Makers painted huge square-shouldered men on the sandstone walls of the canyons. The Pueblos drew snakes and birds and designs like the ones on their pottery. Cave dwellers in Texas made pictures of the sun and the rain, of plumed snakes and giant birds with wings outstretched.

These pictures are cruder than those in Europ[ean]
and African caves. Many of them are n[ot] [much]
better art than the doodles on the margins [of a]
notebook. But they are interesting for the st[ories they]
tell of Indian life. Some are clearly magic — [an ap]-
peal to the sun, a prayer to the rain. Oth[ers seem]
more like an attempt at writing — pictures o[f water]
holes, reports of good hunting or of the trav[els of the]
tribe. For this reason, the American cave a[nd cliff]
paintings are spoken of as *pictographs,* [a word]
meaning "picture writing."

Ancient pictographs on the wall of a cave in Cal[ifornia]

Chapter 8

Exploring Caves

The world's biggest cave room is in Carlsbad Caverns. Mammoth is America's largest cave. —
True or False?

No one is sure of the answer. Every week there are new cave discoveries — no longer accidental discoveries made by boys scrambling down rabbit holes, but carefully planned expeditions, some of which take months of preparation. For cave exploring has become both a science and a popular sport. As a science, it is known as *speleology*.[1] As a sport, it is called *spelunking*.[2]

Not so very long ago these words were unfamiliar. Speleology just didn't exist. Explorers weren't interested in the scientific study of caves. They were too busy trekking through the African jungles or across the ice fields of the Arctic. They were too busy climbing the Alps or sailing the uncharted waters of the South Pacific. Nowadays most of the earth has been explored. The world under the earth is one of the last frontiers.

[1] Say: SPEE-lee-AH-loe-jee.
[2] Say: spee-LUNG-king.

Speleologists haul rope into cave for "mountain climbing."

Still, speleology isn't a brand-new science. It is a combination of many different sciences. It includes geology, of course, and archaeology and biology. It includes surveying and map making and *hydrology*.[3]

Cave hydrologists study the paths of underground waterways. By pouring a harmless green dye into a cave river, they can follow the course of the stream, above and below ground, for many miles. Their work is often of great importance in discover-

[3] Say: hie-DRAH-loe-jee.

ing new sources of water for irrigation and electric power. It can even cause international complications.

At one time Spanish engineers decided to dam up a stream in order to build a power plant on its banks. It was plainly a Spanish stream, and they didn't need to ask any foreigner's permission to do the job. They didn't need to, that is, until a French speleologist, equipped with packets of dye, proved that the Spanish stream flowed through caverns under the Pyrenees Mountains to become the French river Garonne. Damming the stream would have robbed the Garonne of half of its water.

Crossing underground streams and waterfalls is one of the dangers of exploring caves.

Speleology requires more than just scientific knowledge. There are physical hardships and real dangers involved in exploring caves. Speleology requires courage and skill, caution, and — above all — teamwork.

Have you ever heard the story of Floyd Collins? Floyd was a Kentucky farm boy, brought up in cave country. People said Floyd could "smell caves." In 1917, he found the entrance to a cave in his father's front yard. For eight years he spent all of his spare hours under the ground. For days at a time he would disappear, with a kerosene lantern in his hand and a can of beans in his back overalls pocket. When he returned home again, he had tales to tell of enormous rooms, underground rivers, and miles of twisting passageways.

Then came a day when he didn't return home. He'd gone off so often by himself, without saying where he was going or when he would be back, that for a while nobody missed him. Twenty-four hours passed before he was discovered, trapped in a narrow passageway, his foot wedged under a rock that he had dislodged. Rescuers brought him food and blankets, but they were unable to reach the stone that trapped him. All attempts to rescue him failed; and after fourteen days, Floyd Collins died of pneumonia. His body is buried in Crystal Cave, his greatest discovery. Crystal Cave is a monument to bravery, but it is also a warning to those who might foolishly go caving alone.

Floyd Collins Crystal Cave became a commercial cave with three miles of electric lights and footpaths and guardrails. But this was only a small part of the cave. Beyond the lights were the enormous rooms, the underground rivers, and the twisting passageways that Collins had once explored. Did the cave stretch on for ten miles? Or twenty? No one knew.

No one knew, but a group of speleologists were determined to find out. In 1954, twenty-nine years after Floyd Collins' death, sixty-four men and women from all parts of the country traveled to Crystal Cave. A tent city, including a small hospital, kitchen, and a telephone switchboard, was built outside the cave entrance; while an advance party located a campsite under the ground, two miles away. Then came the supply teams bringing in food and medicines, sleeping bags and air mattresses, gasoline for cooking, carbide for lighting, cameras and flash bulbs, nylon ropes and steel ladders, pulleys, drills, jacks, crowbars, compasses, and a rubber life raft. A ton and a half of supplies were pushed and pulled, dragged and carried through the narrow tunnels of the cave. Eight miles of telephone wire and fourteen phones connected the underground camp with the world above.

Doctors and nurses gave physical examinations to each speleologist before he entered the cave. Leaders checked their clothing and equipment: one-piece coveralls and spiked boots, hard hats with carbide lamps clamped on them, knee and elbow pads for the rough crawls, gloves for the rough climbs, flashlights and candles and matches in waterproof containers.

The expedition remained underground for a week, traveling through a maze of tunnels and rooms where no man — not even Floyd Collins — had ever been before. Each member of the team had a job to do, whether it was measuring the air pressure, mapping the new-found passageways, installing telephones, or taking a turn at KP.

Most of the time it was hard work, and dangerous work too. It's difficult to be scientific while wriggling through a hole ten inches wide and fourteen inches high, or walking along the slippery edge of

Crystal Cave expedition came to an end as three members carried out the final load.

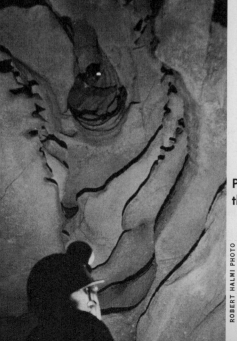

Passages like these challenge the best of cave explorers.

115

a pit that's 100 feet deep. The cavers had to use mountain-climbing equipment to scale steep walls. They had to crawl through the mud and wade through the water. When they returned, they were bearded and bedraggled, with red-rimmed eyes and mud-caked clothes. They squinted at their first sight of the sun in seven days, but there were smiles on their tired faces.

The expedition was a success. There had been no accidents more painful than a cut finger or a bruised knee, no illnesses more serious than a cold or a stomach-ache. Each of the scientists hurried to write up his findings. There were descriptions of blind cave animals, of fossils in the rock, of gypsum flowers and ancient Indian torches. There was even a doctor's report on how people behave when they live in the darkness of a cave for seven days and nights. As for the cave itself, no one talked vaguely any more of "enormous rooms, underground rivers, and miles of twisting passageways." Now there were accurate measurements, photographs, diagrams, maps.

Although this was the largest and best-planned expedition in the history of American cave exploring, it did not succeed in reaching the end of Crystal Cave's crisscrossing tunnels. Other teams have pushed farther and farther under the ground, but even now there are still unexplored passageways. Floyd Collins' cave is certainly one of the largest in the world. The present map of the cave has a total of forty miles of passageways.

Every cave presents a different kind of problem to the explorer. In France, some caves in the mountains are thousands of feet below the surface. The only way to reach them is through narrow, steep shafts. It's like climbing down a well — a well 3,000 feet deep! Sometimes ropes and ladders will do the job, but often electrically operated winches are set up at the entrance. Explorers are harnessed to steel cables and lowered to the cave floor.

In other caves, deep rivers block the passages, and speleologists must use rubber boats and aqualungs to travel from room to room.

Cave exploring has certainly outgrown the kerosene lantern and the can of beans in a back overalls pocket. The National Speleological Society has probably been responsible for many of the changes. Founded in 1939, it is an organization of scientists and sportsmen (including teen-agers who are seven-

These cave explorers in the French Alps reached a level
almost 2,500 feet underground, setting a world record.

teen or older). The Society is systematically studying American caves. Sponsor of the 1954 expeditions to Crystal Cave, it collects all kinds of cave information, from geological reports to the latest in cave headgear or the best way to use an acqualung in an underground river. Its members study blind fish, band bats, and dig up fossil bones. They even fly in airplanes over the limestone hills, looking for cave entranceways.

Most important of all are the Society's DO'S AND DONT'S for cavers:

- Never enter a cave alone.
- Always let someone know where you are going and when you will return.
- Always carry three different lights with you.
- Plan your trip carefully, so that you will have proper clothing and equipment (including a hard hat) and won't get overtired.
- Don't collect cave animal life, nor the stalactites and stalagmites which have been millions of years in the making.

If Floyd Collins had followed these safety rules, he might not have lost his life in a cave.

People have learned a great deal about many subjects since the days of ancient Greece, when men were afraid to enter Pluto's kingdom. Perhaps you think that *everything* has been discovered and that there's nothing left for you to find out. This is not true. That's why speleology is so exciting. There are 12,000 known caves in the United States. Probably there are several times that many still to be discovered.

Here is a study that's just beginning. There is plenty of room for young scientists and explorers in the world under the earth.

Caves to Visit

Alabama:
Cathedral Caverns, *Grant*
Crystal Caverns, *Trussville*

Arizona:
Colossal Cave, *Vail*
Dinosaur Caverns, *Seligman*

Arkansas:
Big Hurricane Cave, *Everton*
Diamond Caverns, *Jasper*
Mystic Cavern, *Marble Falls*
Onyx Cave, *Eureka Springs*
Wonderland Cave, *Bella Vista*

California:
Boyden Cave, *Sequoia National Forest*
Caverns of Mystery, *Shell Beach*
Crystal Cave, *Sequoia National Park, Three Rivers*
Lava Beds National Monument, *Tulelake*
Mercer Caverns, *Murphys*
Mitchell's Caverns State Park, *Essex*
Moaning Cave, *Vallecito*
Pinnacles National Monument, *Pinnacles*
Sea Caves, *La Jolla*

Colorado:
Cave of the Winds, *Manitou Springs*

Florida:
Florida Caverns State Park, *Marianna*

Georgia:
Cave Springs Cave, *Cave Springs*

Idaho:
Craters of the Moon National Monument, *Arco*
Indian Ice Caves, *Shoshone*
Minnetonka Cave, *Paris*

Illinois:
Cave-in-Rock State Park, *Cave-in-Rock*

Indiana:
Donaldson and Twin Cave, *Spring Mill State Park*
Marengo Cave, *Marengo*
Wyandotte Caverns, *Wyandotte*

Jacob's Cave, *Versailles*
Mark Twain Cave, *Hannibal*
Marvel Cave, *Branson*
Meramec Caverns, *Stanton*
Old Spanish Cave, *Reeds Spring*
Onondaga Cave, *Leasburg*
Ozark Caverns, *Camdenton*
Round Spring Caverns, *Round Springs State Park*
Smittle Cave, *Grove Springs*
Stark Caverns, *Eldon*
Montana:
Lewis and Clark Cavern, *near Whitehall*
Nevada:
Lehman Caves National Monument, *Baker*
New Hampshire:
Lost River Glacial Caverns, *North Woodstock*
Polar Caves, *Rumney Depot*
New Mexico:
Carlsbad Caverns, *Carlsbad*
New York:
Adirondack Natural Stone Bridge and Caves, *Pottersville*
Howe Caverns, *Howes Cave*
Secret Caverns, *Howes Cave*
North Carolina:
Linville Caverns, *Ashford*
Ohio:
Crystal Cave, *Put-in-Bay*

Iowa:
Crystal Lake Cave, *Dubuque*
Maquoketa Caves State Park, *Maquoketa*
Wonder Cave, *Decorah*
Kentucky:
Carter Caves State Park, *Olive Hill*
Daniel Boone's Cave, *Nicholasville*
Diamond Caverns, *Park City*
Mammoth Cave National Park, *Mammoth Cave*
Mammoth Onyx Cave, *Horse Cave*
Maine:
Anemone Cave, *Acadia National Park, Bar Harbor*
Maryland:
Crystal Grottoes, *Boonsboro*
Michigan:
Bear Cave, *Buchanan*
Minnesota:
Minnesota Caverns, *Spring Valley*
Mystery Cave, *Spring Valley*
Niagara Cave, *Harmony*
Missouri:
Bridal Cave, *Camdenton*
Crystal Cave, *Springfield*
Fairy Cave, *Reeds Spring*
Fisher's Cave, *Meramec State Park*

Ohio Caverns, *West Liberty*
Seneca Caverns, *Bellevue*
Seven Caves, *Bainbridge*
Zane Caverns, *Bellefontaine*

Oklahoma:
Alabaster Caverns State Park, *Freedom*

Oregon:
Lava River Caves, *Bend*
Oregon Caves National Monument, *near Cave Junction*
Sea Lions Caves, *Florence*

Pennsylvania:
Baker Caverns, *Williamson*
Crystal Cave, *Kutztown*
Historic Indian Caverns, *Spruce Creek*
Indian Echo Cave, *Hummelstown*
Laurel Caverns, *Fairchance*
Lincoln Caverns, *Huntingdon*
Lost Cave, *Hellertown*
Onyx Cave, *Hamburg*
Penn's Cave, *Centre Hall*
Wonderland Caverns, *Mann's Choice*
Woodward Cave, *Woodward*

South Dakota:
Bethlehem Cave, *Bethlehem*
Jewel Cave National Monument, *near Custer*
Rushmore Cave, *Keystone*

Sitting Bull Crystal Caverns, *near Rapid City*
Stage Barn Crystal Caverns, *Piedmont*
Wild Cat Cave, *near Rapid City*
Wild Cave National Park, *Hot Springs*
Wonderland Cave, *Tilford*

Tennessee:
Bristol Caverns, *Bristol*
Cudjo's Cave, *Cumberland Gap*
Cumberland Caverns, *McMinnville*
Jewel Cave, *Dickson*
Lookout Mountain Caves, *Chattanooga*
Tuckaleechee Caverns, *Townsend*
Wonder Cave, *Monteagle*

Texas:
Cascade Caverns, *Boerne*
Caverns of Sonora, *Sonora*
Cave-Without-a-Name, *near Boerne*
Texas Longhorn Cavern, *near Burnet*
Wonder Cave, *San Marcos*

Utah:
Timpanogos Cave National Monument, *near American Fork*

Virginia:
Dixie Caverns, *Salem*

Endless Caverns, *New Market*

Grand Caverns, *Grottoes*

Luray Caverns, *Luray*

Massanutten Caverns, *Harrisonburg*

Melrose Caverns, *Harrisonburg*

Natural Tunnel and Chasm, *near Gate City*

Shenandoah Caverns, *New Market*

Skyline Caverns, *Front Royal*

Washington:

Mount Rainier National Park Ice Caves, *near Longmire*

West Virginia:

Organ Cave, *Huntington*

Seneca Caverns, *Riverton*

Wisconsin:

Cave of the Mounds, *Blue Mounds*

Crystal Cave, *Spring Valley*

Eagle Cave, *Muscoda*

Kickapoo Caverns, *Wauzeka*

Wyoming:

Spirit Mountain Caverns, *Cody*

Index